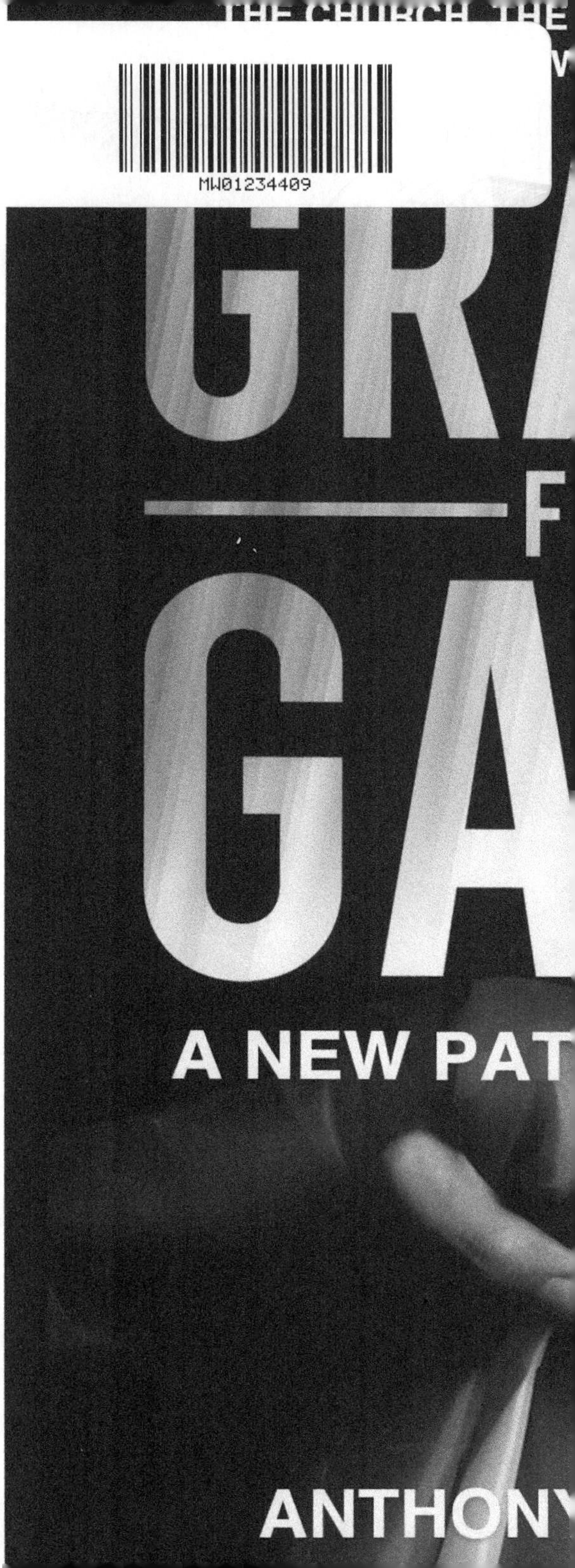
THE CHURCH THE
GR
F
GA
A NEW PAT
ANTHONY

CPSIA information can be obtained
at www.ICGtesting.com
Printed in the USA
BVHW031707191222
654561BV00013B/912

9 780981 554587